Midnight Embers

OTHER BOOKS BY CANDICE JAMES:

A Split In The Water Fiddlehead Poetry Books 1979
Inner Heart – A Journey Silver Bow Publishing 2010
Bridges And Clouds Silver Bow Publishing 2011

Midnight Embers

CANDICE JAMES

libros libertad

First published by:
Libros Libertad Publishing Ltd
2091 140th Street
Surrey, BC, V4A 9V9
Ph. (604) 838-8796
Fax (604) 536-6819
www.libroslibertad.ca

Library and Archives Canada Cataloguing in Publication

James, Candice, 1948-
   Midnight embers : a book of sonnets / Candice James.

ISBN 978-1-926763-22-4

   I. Title.

PS8569.A429M54 2012   C811'.54   C2012-900156-2

Cover Design by Janet Kvammen
Book Layout by SpicaBookDesign

Printed and bound in Canada

ACKNOWLEDGEMENTS:

I would like to thank:

The City of New Westminster for validating my poetry and appointing me *"Poet Laureate"* of this great city.

Michael Sullivan ("Sullivan The Poet") of Plymouth, England for his belief in my sonnets and his constant encouragement. Without his endorsement and genuine interest in my work, this book might never have come to press.

The late Fred Cogswell, BA, MA, PhD, OC, ONB (poet, professor, editor, publisher, literary critic) for publishing my first book ("A Split In The Water" 1979 Fiddlehead Poetry Books) and for believing in me from the very beginning, in the early years.

Richard Doiron, poet, for the time he has spent, tirelessly and sometimes thanklessly, trying to tutor me to write sonnets "the correct way" and for having the patience to tolerate my many "groundless" arguments.

Sharla Cuthberston (daughter) and Emily Cuthbertson (granddaughter) for their unwavering lifelong love and support and for allowing me the time and the space to write and follow my dreams.

Rex Howard who has been a true inspiration to me in both my musical and writing endeavours, standing by me through thick and thin and always being *"the brightest star in my blue heaven"*.

Doug Davidson for inspiring me and encouraging me to start writing again after a long absence from the poetry scene.

Ken Ader for his ongoing support at all my readings, features and events.

Maggie Sanford, Laura Schultz, Janet Kvammen, Bari Barkley, Doreen Bruce, Margit Wagner and the late Julius Caesar Wieser; some of the people who have been a treasure and an influence on me as we have journeyed together, be it a short while or a long while.

And last, but most certainly not least, I would like to thank Manolis Aligizakis and Libros Libertad Publishing for publishing "Midnight Embers, A Book of Sonnets".

To all the wonderful people who have crossed my path and lingered awhile on life's highway with me, I thank you for the joy, the laughter, the smiles and the tears. You have made me who I am today.

Candice James

Table of Contents

"When love is not madness, it is not love."
~Pedro Calderon de la Barca

"A dreamer is one who can only find his way by moonlight, and his punishment is that he sees the dawn before the rest of the world."
~Oscar Wilde

"Love is not dead, that dies again."
~Candice James

Essence

I am the essence of my words today;
A living breathing poem newly born.
If it be worked into a tragic play
Then channelled out in music through a horn
I'll write to recompose myself again
Into a sonnet for the world to read.
To germinate and be blessed by the rain,
Those words that grew so tall from such small seed.
But if by chance this book of me you close
And lay it on the shelf to gather dust,
You'll miss the dew kissed essence of the rose
And all my silver words will turn to rust.

I give to you my essence in this breath;
These living breathing words that know no death.

Sonnet Fever

Poetic dance within itself begins.
Words scramble for positional heartbeat.
They move and groove to rhythm riddled sins.
The dance floor bursts into exceeding heat.
A sonnet fever by another name
Is malady symbolic of the soul.
The symptoms manifest are all the same.
The white is stark, the black as black as coal.
With raging bloodshot eyes that hypnotize
In ever tight'ning vice upon the mind
Insanity doth harness my demise,
As darkened moods continue to unwind.

For sonnet fever, there is no respite.
It writes love's pages at the edge of night.

You Lay Me Down

You lay me down on fields of velvet dreams,
Beneath a ceiling dusted with moon glow;
Then passion's river eddies, swirls and streams
Abducting us into the swift and slow.
Hypnotic rhythms smack lust's slick desire;
Then riding high we spur the red hot steed.
In shafts of moonlight turned to liquid fire,
We're bleeding through the eye of passion's need.
You lay me down again in bed of lies
On sheets of satin stained with glory's blood.
I see my teardrops shining in your eyes.
You hold them back aware my world will flood.

You lay me down and leave me here to burn.
Inside the fragile hope you will return.

Shadow Land

A chanting whisper from love's lost and found
Doth beckon me. I'll chase your ghost tonight.
A haunting memory; I hear the sound
Of voices, shadow dancing with the light.
An aching heart with palpitating beat;
A fevered spirit, racing pulse in wrist;
Desiring flame and your exceeding heat,
That you and I may rise as one in mist.
A brush, a touch, I swear your ghost is near.
A tender kiss, the taste of whiskey breath,
Then I slide down the hard edge of a tear.
Asleep; awake. I shadow box with death,

Where tarnished dreams and crumpled wishes lie,
Inside the shadow land of your goodbye.

Shadow People

The downtown east side streets scream out in pain
In heavy bated breath, in hollow voice;
In desperation drowning in the rain,
Where shadow people live without a choice.
They're strewn and scattered broken bowling pins.
They litter alleys in haphazard spill.
They search for food and clothes in garbage bins.
A cardboard box for shelter in life's swill,
They try to find the crumbling edge of sleep.
They chase their shadows past the point of light,
These broken Cinderellas in too deep;
Prince Charmings zipped inside the cloak of night.

Inside the clutch of hopeless circumstance,
These shadow people never have a chance.

Scarlet Knife

No amnesty within this darkened night
For wounded butterfly in torn cocoon.
Atwist, awry in pallid shaft of light,
Abandoned, dying on a desert dune.
A child of desperation racked with pain
Is sliding down the edge of passion's blade.
A heart is trapped in harsh relentless rain
Where mortal wounds and old scars never fade.
Cut by the sharp tip of love`s scarlet knife,
Heart slaughtered in a boxing ring of tears
Cannot be resurrected back to life.
The promise of forever disappears.

With broken vows laid waste in tattered strings,
Love takes her final leave on tainted wings.

This Destiny

Our body friction feels right flesh to flesh.
It's not too chilly, nor is it too hot.
The mint aroma of your breath, so fresh,
Surrounds my being, penetrates each thought.
Your lips are parted promising new bliss.
In roughest moment laced with violence
You crush my lips 'neath yours in tender kiss.
We've thrown off all disguises and pretense.
We plunge much deeper than we've ever plunged
Rapt in the luscious warmth of love's embrace.
The scent of former lovers now expunged
And all's obliterated save your face.

Born for each other to this destiny;
Eternally locked in love's reverie.

Sudden Thunder

In sacred dark of holy midnight dream,
On feathered down of jet black Raven's wing,
A sparkle shimmers bright in pearl moonbeam.
His heart wide open to what love may bring,
He came to her without pretense or pride.
He laid her down on flower sprinkled bed
That paled against her beauty there beside.
The hours, minutes, seconds rushed ahead,
Lost in the fell clutch of love's sweet embrace.
Nirvana nights, the hazy plush of lust,
He didn't notice changes on her face.
Surprised by sound of sudden thunder thrust,

To pierce his spirit down to marrow's bone;
Soul broken by a pebble love had thrown.

Forest Phoenix

Yes, something lives beneath this deadened ash.
Fire strangled; soil cleansed; life springs anew.
Through ground that's whipped and scarred by Nature's lash
Seeds germinate in charcoal blistered stew.
Evolving remnants of the forest fire,
Charred cones burst open, scatter rife new seed.
Wind rescues them from blazing fune'ral pyre.
This fire that forced a forest to its knees,
Cannot destroy the Phoenix Jack Pine tree.
To rocky face this scorched ground seedling clings.
Indigenous to perpetuity,
Through cold gray ashes, suddenly it springs.

Destroyer wildfire, making forests bleed,
Forgives the Jack Pine and its unborn seed.

Yesterday's Reflections

In thoughts of yesterday, I always find
The wine of lost love mellowed with old age.
It steals across the meadows of my mind;
Our book thus written with unfinished page.
The frost was on the rose. There was no hope.
Abandoned on a dune of crystal snow,
Heart hung on hooks, tied tightly to love's rope,
In fantasy's false land of afterglow.
There be no resurrections. Love is dead,
But mem'ries skulk and wander through my heart,
With feeble insurrections, underfed.
In masquerade's parade the teardrops start:

Emotions, love, affections, poetry
And yesterday's reflections haunting me.

Hollow Man

The hard edged rumour of impending death
Foreshadowing the tragedy at hand;
The heavy muted gasp of bated breath;
Unanswered prayers reign over shadow land.
A paper king trades places with a clown.
An alcoholic drunkard on the town;
A barstool for a throne, smoke for a crown;
And every drink he takes just takes him down.
He can't escape. He has nowhere to go.
Imprisoned in this nightmare of the dead.
A mad fool ruling kingdoms rapt with woe,
Encapsulated in a web of dread.

Addicted and enslaved by his desire
This hollow man that burns in liquor's fire.

Stardust Dreams

Slow tilting windmills dancing to and fro
To wondrous melodies upon the wind;
Forgotten songs we sang so long ago
That neither time nor tide can dare rescind;
Fair rainbow shining on your cherished face
Illuminating shadows and showdowns;
With bleeding feet I still will stay the race.
The weeping clowns' smiles fading into frowns
Will turn to joy again when you return.
With stardust dreams spilled out from midnight's pail,
A smould'ring moonbeam will enflame and burn,
To kiss the mystic waters we will sail.

Embracing passion, with each touch and breath,
We'll dance forever past the point of death.

Daybreak

New dawn awakens, shakes off evening's dust.
The sun unzips and morning's light breaks through.
A flower opens in a show of trust.
God's voice, at first a whisper, on the dew,
As sunshine spills out over mountain peak.
The Royal City bathed in regal crown.
A robin in a treetop primps to speak
A lilting song to wake the sleeping town.
The city poses in a polished glow,
A rainbow painting mirroring its heart.
It dances to its rhythmic undertow
In circle with no middle end or start.

Then daylight's once again brought to its knees
When twilight's fingers start to flex then squeeze.

Perfect Smile

To gaze upon your face brings sorrow's end;
To see your eyes light up when I arrive;
On angel's wings to heaven I ascend.
My heartbeat quickens as it comes alive.
I love to hear you whispering my name.
It writes new symphonies within my heart.
You touch my hand and embers turn to flame.
You flow through me and fill up every part.
As you move softly into my embrace
My lips are parted, hungry for your kiss.
I trace the lines of love upon your face
And know there is no greater joy than this.

I pledge to tarry with you all the while;
To live and die within your perfect smile.

Wanton Dream

Moon shadows boxing on a starlit sea,
In ring of darkened water set aflame;
These sparring beasts fight nightly, endlessly
To no avail. There's no redemption, fame.
Afire in ropes of karma's penitence
They try in vain to fly with shredded wings.
Spills softly from the sky in reverence,
Eternity's torn bag of needful things.
Crushed dreams, dark hope, are trapped in static time.
Lost angels, demons grip the edge of fear,
As whispers echo, ghostly pantomime,
Disguised in smiles parading through a tear.

Emotions rife and ripping at the seam,
I choke on screams inside this wanton dream.

Fate

He shuts his eyes and flies through stars above.
He grabs the wind with fingers of his mind.
He zips himself in midnight's satin glove
To watch the threads of time as they unwind.
He wonders, nights, how many days are left
Before the candle's wick burns down to ash.
The best of love and flame lost and bereft.
Gone with the pan where first he saw them flash.
The end is near his life runs like a reel.
A guilty sinner chiding innocence,
Too late to change his wicked ways and steal
A yesterday to trade for recompense.

Alas he fears he cannot change his state.
He's Karma's prey accursed.   He can't cheat fate.

This Tree

*(As a child I played in Queen's Park New Westminster, BC
and still today I love to visit this beautiful park and sit under that
same old tree I've sat under through childhood's page, middle age and
the golden years)*

In silence stands a tree that's always been.
With love's initials carved into her bark.
Through seasonal and changing shades of green
The fingerprints of time have left their mark.
She's home to Robins, Wrens and Stellar Jays
And lovers lost in languished sweet embrace.
In childhood, teenage days and adult plays,
She's witnessed smiles and tears upon my face.
I've watched her dance in every season's arms;
In nakedness and wrapped in shiny leaves.
I've seen her swoon, fall prey to Autumn's charms,
And watched the dying leaves fall from her sleeves.

A sentinel on guard that's always been,
This tree has eyes and oh, the sights she's seen!

Collision

The fireworks splash on sky of ebony;
Night's edges burning down to raw red dawn.
Our compass broken so we wandered free
With nothing left of value we could pawn.
We trusted in the knowledge of the wind
And drifted on the wet silk of her lip,
Until our vows of love we did rescind.
Untangled heartbeats; disjoined at the hip.
To out of style forgotten melodies,
We spun beneath the axis of the moon.
Two comets burning passion to its knees,
We fell from midnight crashing into noon.

Collision of these comets now erased,
We're antiquated sonnets thus defaced.

Full Circle

The frost was on the rose. There was no hope.
Abandoned on a dune of crystal snow,
He dug his boots in. He would scale this slope
For ember burning in love's afterglow.
A damp and dismal cold, chilled to the bone.
He turned his collar to the wind once more.
A heavy heart, a statue made of stone,
Now trapped in squalid storm on distant shore.
He swept the ice and teardrops from his eyes
To focus on her misty silhouette.
She swayed in fog at edge of mountain's rise,
A ballerina dancing pirouette.

His heartbeat pounding faster in his chest;
Fate came full circle, danced her to his breast.

Darkness Undressing

There is no consolation in this lie
That spills from lips to save me from heartbreak.
There is no soft edge to this hardened sigh
That begs the angels, destiny forsake.
The promise of forever fleeing fast;
The well worn, stale and frayed ties binding us;
Our hearts and bowed heads praying to the past
Believing in forgiveness finding us.
In bearing witness to the dark undressed
A butterfly cocoon turns inside out.
Now handcuffed, shackled to our lust unblessed,
We balance on the shadow of a doubt.

Love kneels in vain and begs one final dance;
Alas, no rescue for this dead romance.

Naked and Needing

A wet moon spilling, hanging in the sky.
It waxes shining through the edge of night;
A shimm'ring snowball, brilliant gleaming eye,
It slays the dark with swords of bleached white light.
A shining hero framed in ebony;
Unholy moments casting off their shame
Fulfilling karmic quest and destiny.
We hear the heaven's calling out our name.
A sad sonata written on the sleeve
Of angels' wings to star dust satin night,
Entwining souls and making us believe
Our hearts have wings thus we begin our flight.

We strip the layers off our bleeding souls,
In naked needing as the thunder rolls.

Quicksilver!

A rainbow prism image glints and shines
As silver sleet is dressing up the streets.
The asphalt, dotted white in zebra lines;
Gun metal sky rains bullets down in sheets.
Old wounds break open slicing glossy night.
A shoddy dream's abandoned to cruel fate.
Behind cracked key holes curtains are drawn tight.
As I slay dragons outside heaven's gate,
I brandish wisdom high as my sword cuts
This savage tiger chewing at my thoughts.
Behind a rusty door my jailer shuts
Old Cinderella tales that stole new plots.

Quicksilver! Passion's soul mate comes and goes
Like hoar frost on the grass, dew on the rose.

Eternal

Hushed whispers flow with love through my phone line.
And yesterday lives on though it's been lost.
Your voice so bittersweet warms like fine wine.
Would we have loved if we had known the cost?
Would we dare try to resurrect our past?
No heart could twice endure so great a pain.
Still waters running deep pass by too fast.
Our yesterday will never come again.
Lost in the pause between heartbeats and sighs.
It's floating in love's sediment of tears.
We vow our love again in tender lies;
The embers burning through the passing years.

So good to hear your voice inside this rain;
To know I'm still on your soul like a stain.

Kerala

Old stone age carvings in Edakkal Caves;
A spirit's voice is whisp'ring. Hear it call;
A glint of glory crashing through the waves
Of prehistoric wonder's waterfall.
Mudskippers, crabs, frogs, striking cormorants;
The darters, turtles, spotted otters splash;
The Palm trees, Pandas, caterpillars, ants
Survey this shoreline, brushed with brilliant flash.
Small ponds, canals, blue lakes and waterways;
Lush back woods trails and brackish green lagoons
The painted sunsets blinking out the days
And then the daunting rush of dark monsoons.

God's land of beauty, song and history,
Kerala, land of love and mystery!

Hope

Crushed fragments, shards of soul still left alive;
Iconoclast now gasping its last breath
For sons and daughters that did not arrive.
No use to fight. We all succumb to death.
Foundations built on weak and shifting sand;
Imprisoned in a life that can't hold us,
We'll find firm footing in the promise land.
If we believe the words the Lord told us,
And if by faith we vanquish every doubt,
He'll brandish truth to guide us through life's maze.
He'll light a flame that no one can put out.
From now until eternal end of days

We'll fly through rainbows of enlightenment
To every corner in His firmament.

Sun Shadows

Sun shadows jump and chase the fading light
Through dampened down of dreams left in rain,
As glowing embers paint the edge of night,
A sugar, candy coloured, coral stain.
A bittersweet refrain calls from the deep.
A heartache wakens chanting out my name,
No longer buried, and no more asleep,
In dark disguises hiding from the shame.
Now Injury's unshackled from insult
To Second guess an old emotion's pain.
I can't avoid but come to same result.
I realize you'll never come again.

Sad stories dance in shafts of pale moonlight;
Sun shadows chasing stars at edge of night.

The Whistler

The whistler wanders graveyards late at night.
He whispers haunting eerie melody.
He hides in shadows cast by fading light.
A threat'ning figure skulking fleetingly,
He feigns non sequiturs, so sweet and low.
He lures lost, wounded souls into his snare.
His victims line death's doorway row on row.
A dangerous acquaintance should fools dare
To grasp his hand when lost in creeping fog.
He chews their mem'ries, dining on their soul,
This mascot straight from Hell, mad demon dog,
Has heart as dark as night, eyes black as coal.

The whistler hides at darkened edge of night.
He cannot touch those walking in the light.

Sundrenched

Thoughts, backward cast upon old sundrenched days,
Unwind in darkened corners of my mind.
Romantic ships set sail on twilight's haze
With bittersweet tears floating close behind.
Then embers from the past burst into flame.
As maudlin moonlight drifts through swaying trees.
It thaws the icicles off each freeze frame.
A whispered love song on an errant breeze
Sees love's caress cool on lust's fevered brow:
Before two puppet lovers broke their string;
Before time escalated then to now;
Before they felt the harsh whip of love's sting.

The sundrenched days have lain down in the rain.
With echoes, pain and heartaches they'll remain.

Smooth Stone

The slow and surly turn of lovers' smiles
To curled up lips that aim barbs at the heart
Though we'd rehash these last past million miles
It still would come to this. We'd have to part.
Perhaps we should have flipped a shiny dime
Or made a wish we knew could not come true.
There is no measurement to fit this crime.
We should have chased the horse that threw his shoe.
On precipice of love's unbalanced ledge
With canyons deep and shrapnel all around
I've nothing left to lose; no bet to hedge,
To claim a righteous slice of solid ground.

Tonight I stand at edge of night alone
And skip love's water like a smooth, smooth stone.

The Gift

My fingertips have brushed the cheek of love.
I've sparred and boxed with tears I could not smite.
I've felt their essence through bruised satin glove;
Been wrapped in passion burning down the night.
In all its splendour, true love is a jewel;
A precious diamond that outshines fool's gold;
A sacred sword that flays and slays the cruel;
Its value priceless; can't be bought or sold.
The best of life is always given free.
A kiss from loved ones and a baby's smile;
These things remain throughout eternity.
True love and passion never out of style.

Though Earth and all its pleasures pass away
The greatest gift, true love, is here to stay.

Rain Painting

We traveled further from receding sleep
In sheets of rapture ripped by lust's embrace.
We sojourned 'long side danger in the deep
Like drifters disappearing without trace.
We touched the razor that forbade escape
And wore the scars of one too many starts.
Our tears were abstract, paint we couldn't scrape
Off broken dreams and battered virgin hearts.
We faced the truth, unwrapped our tender lies
And held them to the light so we could see
Hell's angels wearing heaven's best disguise;
The razor's ecstasy now agony:

An ink stained letter wracked with love and pain;
Unrecognizable left in the rain.

Psychosis

Inside this darkened paradigm of doom,
Where paranoia's zealot speaks in tongues,
Damp ghostly whispers drown this floating room.
Old worn, torn safety nets, strung without rungs
Crack ears beneath the sharp edged screech of bats.
Dark spectres traipsing through horrific nights
Pass frowning clowns in corners changing hats.
Gorillas chase down tigers flying kites.
Enveloped in high frequency white noise,
Walls shake, vibrate lamenting of the dead.
Death's lost its sting and I have lost my voice.
No gallows for these demons in my head,

With hearts as hard as steel, eyes black as coal;
They rend the essence of my tattered soul.

Suddenly

You suddenly appeared before my eyes.
It didn't feel the way I thought it would.
Where did they go, those passion flavoured sighs?
Where is the pedestal on which you stood?
A second hand emotion broke and bent
That holds no trace of us that's not unblessed
Just panorama clips of love misspent.
There were too many sins left unconfessed.
Today I looked hard in your eyes to see
A sparkle hiding somewhere in your heart,
But in your eyes I saw no trace of me
So now at last I leave this tragedy.

Today I saw how much I meant to you;
No more than passing glint of morning dew.

Death's Shadow

He's stands on guard, forever vigilant.
The edge of night is creeping, closing in.
He searches shadows cold and indigent.
Unshackled in Pandora's box of sin,
He hears the rattle rale of ancient bones.
They clamour, echo, scream incessantly.
In atmosphere filled with horrific moans
They claw with tooth and nail to be set free.
Inside this prison born of misplaced trust,
Harsh deeds and sins too monstrous to deny.
The clamour of a ghost disturbing dust,
With jangling keychain counting tears gone by.

His eyelids shut. The keys fall to the floor.
Defying life, Death's shadow locks the door.

Weep Not

The mountains up ahead don't wear me out.
It's that small grain of sand stuck in my shoe.
I've been around and know love's turnabout.
There is no exit. All roads lead to you.
I'm plagued with fever of emotion's ills
And burdened with intentions gone astray;
Adrift and drowning in tsunami swills
Where broken hearts and dreams are swept away.
My Epitaph shall be inscribed in stone.
"She swam in waters dark, beyond her depth.
With broken heart, her ghost remains alone;
Forever haunted by love's dying breath."

Weep not for me or for my saddened state.
I made the choice although I knew my fate.

Ghostly Tryst

Rhiannon's ghost lurks in the moor's cloyed mists.
The champing steed rears up and snorts alarm.
The horseman grips the reins in tightened fists,
He draws his sword to ward off pending harm.
It glistens bright in shaft of pearl moonbeam.
An ancient lost marauder's heart of steel,
Is trapped in claws of lust's recurring dream,
A demon dog is nipping at his heel.
Rhiannon snares him in her cold embrace.
Her passion thrusting deep into his bone;
Time disappears, reversing inner space;
Old embers turn to ashes; hearts to stone.

Beneath a dark sky, shackled at the wrist
Hell's witch and horseman lie in ghostly tryst.

Philosopher's Stone

Sad, disenfranchised existentialist,
Divorced from all responsibilities;
Despairing, ling'ring in horizon's mist.
Bent spirit crippled with fragilities,
No more subjective to the human state,
But yet subjunctive to the written word.
Papyrus stapled to magnetic slate;
A composition, sacrosanct, unheard.
Philosophizing past the "nth" degree
Man's freedom, pain, religion and belief.
The question is to be, or not to be.
The answer, filched by deaf mute and blind thief.

The secrets of philosopher's gem stone,
In fate's lips sealed and with the angels flown.

White

These sleeping giants in frostbitten jaw;
White soldiers standing guard beyond the shore,
Where ice meets ocean, polar bear and claw,
And Neptune's floor holds hands with heaven's door.
A creaking whine, the crunch of iceberg's scrape;
The echo of a timber wolf's sharp keen
That pierces silent, stark, and bleached landscape,
Unmarked by footprints, virgin and pristine.
The Arctic Fox, and Orcas black and white,
The Snowy Owl in sanctuary's nest
Held under tongue of winter's icy bite,
Lost to the taste of dew on Spring time's breast.

A moon shone masterpiece in snowy white;
A Rembrandt painting pearled in shafts of bright.

The Fall

In tangled tango, two hearts chose to dance.
We burned the candle, lit both ends aflame.
I knew the danger but still took the chance;
Became a loser in love's no win game.
The love light dimmed and faded out of sight.
I watched my dreams grow old and turn to rust.
You weren't my Knight in shining armour bright
And I was not your gold beneath the dust
But still your image creeps into my mind
Dissolving into tears that burn my cheek.
Too many midnights I wake up and find
A strangled prayer that rises but won't speak.

I knew right from the start I'd lose it all,
But I still played the game and took the fall.

Hologram

A torrid blazing sun waxed ever bright
In supernova of dimension far.
The little clouds climb up to dizzied height,
On laddered dust, ascending to a star,
Past where the White Dove and the Eagle fly;
Cascading mem'ries from midnight to dawn
They wink and blink through drooped and wat'ry eye;
Their hist'ry, myst'ry, buried, but not gone;
Time's pages musty, windblown, passing by,
On star dust's sacred air and angel's breath,
Eliciting wry smile, and glist'ning eye,
To shrink the border lines of life and death.

We live and breathe this Karmic epigram,
Caught in the clutch of surreal hologram.

Great Sorrow

There is great sorrow when you lose your way.
Past deeds still echo and reverberate
With symbolism, much to my dismay,
And I'm unable to escape this state.
The world's askew and life has turned askance,
It spirals inward to my heart's demise.
Now lost in sorrow, locked inside this trance,
New oceans swell and deepen in my eyes.
But given one more chance to choose again
I'd have the dance. I wouldn't sit it out.
I'd still walk down that road and bear the pain
That passion dishes out in turnabout.

I couldn't heed my inner warning voice,
Abstruse heart didn't leave me any choice.

King Of Silver Sonnets

The silver sonnet king is stoking flames
With words that flow like honey flavoured wine.
He waltzes them through new poetic games
In harmonies that dance with rhythmic line,
He weaves each word with master tailor's thread;
And stitches feelings to them seamlessly;
Like spiced rum spilled by sailor at mast head,
That's effortlessly dried by windy sea.
He visits bright days, from the edge of dark.
Strict jurist, judge and executioner
He lolls in zoo pool, such a well fed shark,
And spins sweet metaphors of blood and myrrh.

The king of silver sonnets never dies!
In ling'ring verses, elegant, he lies.

Trickster

Come closer trickster shadowing my soul
With residue of lust and passion's burn.
I walk into your eyes as black as coal,
Down darkened alleys off'ring no return.
A wordsmith, man of letters thus renowned;
Death's swordsman clinging to lost innocence;
You speak in riddles, echoing false sound.
Dead to the past, a ghost in present tense,
Resewing edges torn by distant death.
You climb each mountain on its steepened rise;
And kill me softly with your bated breath,
Embracing death, I dive into your eyes

To glean the glint of your hard hearted stare,
And then perhaps to strip your conscience bare.

Dark Side Of Black

A dark side demon somewhere here resides.
It chains my wrists to darkest shade of black.
On battered barbed wire broken ocean tides,
That flow from hell through deepened crevice crack,
It claws my scalp, and drills into my skull.
Tranquility transformed to raw red bones,
Exposing blood inside this foggy dull;
Archaic slaughters in forbidden zones;
Their nexus piercing, ringing Saturn's trine
A gnash of teeth chew holes into my bust.
Lust's mutiny commanding by design
My heart is flayed to bloodied crumbling dust.

On darkest side of black I lick my lips,
And tremble under masochistic whips.

Sinners' Sea

Unbalanced barefoot at the edge of hell;
Just holding on, with barbed wire cutting deep;
He gazed down where misfortune's Divas fell
In blackened pit known as the Devil's Keep.
He entered Black Jack's house of plastic cards.
He took the dive, let chips fall where they may,
And sought out blessings from poetic bards
Whose poetry was born of tragic play.
He tossed the dice, threw caution to the wind;
Saw devils grin and rub their horns with glee.
In arrogance he ventured he might win,
Though he'd been written in Hell's history.

Too late to beg repentance, such as he,
Was born to swim with sharks in sinners' sea.

New Westminster

White specks that glow amidst the amber shine
On charcoal tapestry that hangs above.
Like sparkling diamonds sprinkled on skyline,
A chandelier of stars adorns night's glove.
Inherent music written and thus pinned,
As dreams fall softly from an angel's sleeve,
Unspooling on a gentle evening wind,
And spilling magic wishes from its weave.
A touch of glory, magic in the air;
A footprint on life's water and the earth;
A drifting hush of mem'ries everywhere;
A whisp'ring wind; A diamond of great worth.

The Royal City's crowned in glossy light
As New Westminster shines the edge of night.

Interference Pattern

The book of me was written years ago
When I was but a glint in father's eye;
The child he'd come to sire but never know;
Too much alike and still the twain too shy.
I'm trapped inside this antiquated dream
Of trepidation's holographic fate
That tries to suffocate my primal scream.
I find no mercy, for my wretched state.
Before I leave I'll look in on myself
To see if I was ever really there.
I'll place the book of me high on hell's shelf
That no one else may dare this nightmare share.

I know I am not here. I must be there;
Just drifting, interference patterned air.

Tool And Die

To fugitive I've jailed inside my soul:
I've thrown the locks that you may now escape.
I've tooled the wall with gaping three foot hole,
Destroyed all traces of police red tape.
I've turned my back. My eyes won't see you go,
If surreptitiously you choose to leave.
It matters not I've nothing left to show
Except a broken heart that still will grieve.
So many wasted nights spent guarding love
When it was just illusion from the start.
Magician, dressed in black hat and silk glove,
Do one last trick and give me back my heart.

So fugitive run hard. You must run fast.
Destruction's stamped you and the die is cast.

Nemesis

I sit here talking Captain Morgan jive,
My tongue is loosed by pull of spicy rum;
I sip the music up and come alive
Then beetle down inside a droning hum,
The room starts spinning, old ghosts pass me by.
I smile at each and proffer all a wink;
Though most are surly, one gives me the eye
Nirvana's caught in never ending blink.
It's Tweedle Dum as is to Tweedle Dee.
The barroom drunks now reeling, yell and hiss,
In cacophony's harshest harmony
But I'm oblivious with whiskey kiss.

We're setting sail for serendipity,
My nemesis, that Morgan lad and me.

Giggle Damned Moment

The blood licked sacrilege of dark torn night
Doth feast on sleeping demon much maligned.
In blood and black lace, resurrection's plight
Leaves shady fingerprints where devils dined.
A quicksand mire is wrapping round my feet,
I'm sucked down through the depths of dark despair.
My soul is smacked by flame's exceeding heat.
Fire's holocaust is fixed in hollow glare.
Insanity is paired with sanity:
They two step on disaster's floor as one.
They wink at me and scream profanity.
They watch my life unravel, come undone.

I'm jailed inside this giggle damned event,
And wrapped in chunks of spirit, skewed and bent.

Burman, A Legacy

a tribute to Raoul Dev Burman - June 27, 1939 –January 4, 1994
*commonly known as **R. D. Burman**, nicknamed **Pancham**,*
he was one of India's greatest music composers.

A rainbowed angel sings a brand new song;
With tender notes and sweet seraphim wine;
Intoxication flowing fast and strong
While Burman and his composition dine.
On pristine diamonds sewn on angels' wings;
In moon shade glowing bright with cosmic dust;
Imagination, baptized, rings and sings;
Embraces white light with encircling trust;
It blends the tragic, magic in his veins;
He scores his epitaph on music's door;
He writes his history in bold refrains
A living legacy forevermore.

We hear his songs on winds, in rustling leaves,
And though he's dead, he is not dead. He breathes.

Dimensionalization

Could I be but a structured form of paste
Discarnate, yet believing I exist?
A spirit in a state of hybrid grace;
In actuality just moving mist.
Am I a portal to the other side
Or mortal merely biding, chiding time?
My spirit's breath can never be denied
Its perfect rhythm interlaced with rhyme.
My structured form continues changing face
I run amongst the stars chased by the moon;
Where time and fate insist on trading space
And journey's end, as always, comes too soon.

Dimensionalization blurs my eyes
As soul moves from disguise to new disguise.

Distant Thunder

Reborn believers hoisting love's sail high
On raging, torrid sea of Babylon,
We flew on feathered breath of angel's sigh,
Through heaven's harmony from dusk till dawn.
Encrypted hieroglyphic messages
Carved scarlet lettered scent straight from your soul
On satin sheets, enraptured vestiges.
We were the ones for whom the bell would toll.
Amid the throes of passion's heated kiss
I felt your tight embrace begin to slip.
And looking back remember only this;
Your face fast fading on another ship.

Now put asunder flavour of the day,
As love like distant thunder fades away.

Reckoning

A chorus of Seraphim Cherubs sing,
While Heaven echoes resonating sighs,
With dewdrops shining bright on rainbow wing.
In golden garments, diamond studded eyes,
The Holy of the Holiest white light;
In reverence I kneel beside the dead.
The light expands illuminating bright.
The book of life in loud clear voice is read.
I tremble praying my name's found in it;
Then thunder, lighting as the dead arose.
A number carved on forehead brows was writ.
As demons danced in Hellish lustful throes;

The sinners snatched away by dev'lish throng
While saints stayed swaying rapt in Angels' song.

Tide

I drew a straight line on the dampened sand,
Stood back and measured all the things you'd done;
Tossed lies and tears to sea and made my stand.
Before they drowned they glinted in the sun.
I heard them moaning, groaning out your name.
I almost crossed the line to save love's soul;
Then I remembered you're the one to blame
For hard edged nights that daily took their toll.
The tide was threat'ning to erase my line.
I scarce could bear to watch it wash away,
But wash away it did, and left no sign
Of love you took away that fateful day.

The tide has drowned the past. I now must face,
Though once we loved, today there is no trace.

Disenfranchised

Now disenfranchised from your wanton heart
I beg to reconcile our falling out
Of paradise before it fell apart.
Cut into hard edged shadows of a doubt
I could not cling to reassuring pleas.
Accusatory tones crept in my voice.
They broke love's back and drove it to its knees.
Your false and wounded pride left you no choice.
You left me in the lurch and went to her
But in your eyes I see old embers burn.
We can't erase the debt love doth incur.
I wait anticipating your return

To disenfranchise every tear that drops
And blend our heartbeats 'til the day mine stops.

The Fool

Exposures doubled down in magic stills
Still haunt my mind with no respite in sight.
Your fingerprints embossed by love's sharp quills
Igniting songs that burn the edge of night.
I guess you loved me in your selfish way
But I played second fiddle in your heart;
An unimportant extra in your play.
You were the star. I had a minor part.
Yes you were always standing centre stage.
You strutted, voice commanding loud and clear
And tried to hide your bitterness and rage
Inside the hard edged rumour of a tear.

The depth and essence of your heart deride
The measure of the fool who lives inside.

Mem'ry's Boat

The Sun is forcing drapes to crack like ice
To whet the edge of passion's aftermath.
Sensational, a tasty slice of spice,
As mem'ry's boat floats kisses in the bath
On hazy dreams that once recalled our names.
Abducted in a flash without a trace,
Left searching for a breath to fan the flames,
We chase the moon with sunburnt heart and face;
And search the vast expanse of bed between
Two lonely lovers. We've seen better days.
The cupboard's bare. Our hearts have grown so lean.
Love takes her leave in afterburn of blaze.

The Sun dissolves; the curtains droop and fall
On pools of tears where lovers once stood tall.

Beyond Belief

I'm walking down a trail of broken hearts
Where shadows haunt and taunt my sordid soul.
A grimaced tale of woe each face imparts.
A cloud burst breaks. I hear the thunder roll.
I turn my collar up to choke the wind
The truth, so hard to come by, fills my eyes.
Each lovely lie I told, I do rescind,
Although this does not soften love's demise.
But if your heart should have a change of mind
To suffer love's forgiveness for my sake,
And if the hand of fate has thus designed,
Then from this hellish nightmare I will wake,

To leave at last this shadow land of grief
And die with you in bliss beyond belief.

Sun Slice

The Sun is slicing through the mountain's crest,
Reflecting like a dream through heaven's eyes;
To search your soul, your heart, your wanton breast.
The air I sucked was softer than your sighs.
I spent my hours drifting on your smile;
We navigated love all season long
And sang of pyramids along the Nile.
You were the music and I was the song.
Then draped the fabric of a colder night
Across the unsuspecting torrid day.
My compass shattered in the waning light.
On darkened lake I felt you slip away.

I'll find you at the sun sliced edge of night
And dance with you again 'neath heaven's light.

Streetlamp Glow

Beneath the buttered ball of streetlamp glow
A solitary figure sheds a tear;
And I, a stranger passing by, still know
Her depth of sorrow and her greatest fear.
Sheer madness running rampant fills the air.
It permeates the essence of her core.
But for the grace of God I could stand there
In her same shoes where I have stood before.
We whispered to a wind that didn't hear.
We begged to be forgiven, taken home.
We called out to a man with deafened ear,
Who left us nothing but a fine tooth comb.

Our tears stream down. A river starts to flow
Beneath the buttered ball of streetlamp glow.

False Promise

A bird perched on the brim of pirate time,
A flightless albatross at rusted wheel
And crusty captain's bready eyes of steel
Still sail on seven seas of reaper's rhyme.
A glint in sun baked world of rolling hell,
With torn and tattered sail hung down in shred,
Half mast and anchored to respect the dead,
Adrift on endless wave of ocean swell;
Then of a sudden storm clouds drifted in.
Metallic charcoal filled the outcast sky
But no respite for dry or arid eye;
A false forgiveness of unuttered sin.

Then demon sun arose from sleep again,
Rescinding her false promise of the rain.

Pernicious Moon

Pernicious and precocious fading moon,
A shaft of broken glass to pierce my heart;
And further from my eyes it will not part
Although it knows the sun will crash through noon.
At first it shimmers with a pearly glow
Then hides its face behind a cloud in shame
In hope of casting off unwanted blame
When love's bow breaks and falls on hearts below.
But if a heart has strong enough belief
Perhaps a star will spill some magic dust
On lovers' vows the years have turned to rust
And turn back time to when there was no grief.

Pernicious moon no longer to parade
In handcuffs joined to sorrow's masquerade.

Poltroon

Poltroon, in trance was perched on boulder tall,
Reciting poetry from long ago.
The legend of a cold and callous fall
Of star crossed lovers cast in shadow glow.
A spectre hawk rose from his aerie high
To latch his claws upon poltroon's thin skin.
In fear of lightning bolt from yonder sky
Dug deeper ripping flesh that rots within;
The hawk lost grasp then gust of wind blew hard
At ope'ning of the latent eye of third.
The hawk took flight. Poltroon left marked and scarred,
Hurled hard a prayer to wing of demon bird,

And wounded hawk flew crippled to the moon
Reflecting in the eyes of lost poltroon.

The Search

Oh man of many lives, and sacred smiles,
I've searched this endless universe for you.
I've roamed the many multitudes of miles,
When seas were old and mountains rising new.
I chased your ghost through hazy nights and days
From north to south, to star, from ship to shore.
I danced with shadows in a million plays,
Where dreams and magic mixed with days of yore.
No, never strangers, souls sewn at the seams.
Our paths had crossed forever and again,
When oceans were just bubbling newborn streams
And dreams were dust and glory rapt in rain.

You'll reappear from pages of our past,
And passion's flame will be relit at last.

Branding Irons

At times I fear you and your source of tears,
Jewels trickling down the cheek of yesterday.
A hazy memory that spans the years
Commands the starring role in passion's play.
You blend your evil with majestic spark.
I'm hypnotized by embers as they fade,
Magnificently at the edge of dark,
In guise of primal, fevered masquerade.
You've tied me to the secrets in your heart
That hide inside your blood so cleverly.
Not even death can pull we two apart.
Our hearts and souls are burning. Look and see!

Behold! Our hands are branding irons, hot coal;
And with one touch we brand each other's soul.

Found

The thirst is over, throat now fully slaked.
In silence, soothingly and savagely,
My heart warmed in love's oven, slowly baked.
I've waited years for your return to me.
This hunger born of lust that must be done,
A dormant fire that only you can light,
To burn a hotter flame than boasts the Sun.
Now you've returned to end this endless night.
I crumble, die inside your arms again.
The rumpled sheets, they sweat beneath our weight.
Lust kills the cold and passion kills the pain.
Love's destiny has kept her date with fate.

Last night the truth of love came shining through
I found myself when I was lost in you.

Crab Cakes, Jazz And You

Those sparkling lusty nights at Java Jazz
We slow danced close as Salvè sang her soul;
And Eddie played the sweetest razzmatazz
As we held hands in amber candle glow.
And there we were reflecting in love's eyes
The lovelight, music, dancing, and crab cakes
Today life weaves the fabric of my sighs
Each night in dreams before the dream awakes.
But if I think on crab cakes, jazz and you
Those magic melodies engulf my heart
Then yesterday appears in shades of blue.
And brings the same old thrill as at the start.

There are some feelings even time can't kill.
I loved you then and now. I always will.

Glossy Nights

A soft caress of windblown drizzling breeze;
The headlights shimmer, pearl on silky black;
Their gloss evokes a midnight sizzling freeze.
The traffic lights shoot arrows from their sack,
A glist'ning, gleaming, flaring matchstick tide
On rain slicked streets that shine this glossy town.
Night wizard's bag of tricks now opens wide.
A magic show of shooting stars pitch down
Burnt buttered arrow slabs from quiv'ring bow.
I hear a voice. Your ghost calls out to me
Through empty alley's amber candle glow,
Illuminating pathways to the Quay.

Your ghostly nuzzle's sealed inside a kiss;
Oh how I live for glossy nights like this.

Poor Butterfly

Reflections pool and ripple in my eyes.
A glimpse of yesterday comes to the fore.
Then falls a teardrop dripping wet with sighs.
Still searching for the key to heaven's door,
I creep like fog along this lonely street.
There be no greater curse than lover's scorn.
The night crawls by on caterpillar feet;
Poor butterfly that never will be born.
Anachronism unto my own death,
Imprisoned, cuffed by yesterday's sweet kiss,
Reliving each caress and urgent breath,
Your memory holds court on nights like this.

This flame of love, although 'tis much maligned,
Still flickers in the corners of my mind.

January Snow

On winds of change I flew on wings of chance
In search of brighter flames that I could light
And sweeter music begging me to dance.
On broken wings, a bird in maiden flight,
I could not navigate. I lost my way.
The fires I lit too soon succumbed to dark.
They burned to ashes, empty, cold and gray.
And gone the glint of ember's dying spark,
No flicker left of love's chilled aftermath;
Just tears and fears that huddle in the heart;
And every dream has drowned in tepid bath.
Each night grows darker since we've been apart.

On fragile days and nights, love's afterglow
Is colder than the January snow.

Afterburn

If I could see you now, how would I feel?
Would old emotions stir in me again?
Would touch of flesh and fire once more reveal
That from this drug of lust I can't abstain?
Would I be yours again to brutalize
By crush of hard edged kiss upon my breast?
Would wanton lips begin to tantalize?
With blessings sought before the sin's confessed?
Our bridges burned and crumbled long ago
And now a raging river runs between
The two of us and who are we to know
Or even try to guess what might have been?

If I could see you now would love return?
No, one can't light a flame in afterburn

There Are Songs

I wave goodbye to urchins from my past.
They squeal with great delight as I depart,
But there are tear filled ghosts before the mast
Lamenting my departure with sad heart.
I whisper low in trepidation's hall
Well hidden from the wild and woolly throng.
I drift above the edge of Autumn's fall
And hum forgotten yet familiar song
Vibrating softly on a stranger's lips.
I can't quite grasp its name from memory.
It's almost there and then its essence slips,
But always it reminds of you and me.

Yes, there are songs, and there are songs sung blue,
But none so sweet as those I sang with you.

Nevada Evenings

I close my eyes. I'm in your arms again.
Nevada evenings, sun is sinking low,
Unwrapped in glow of tepid desert rain.
Two lovers in Mojave sunset glow;
An airplane flying sideways on a sigh,
Distilling mem'ries, tears in twilight skies;
On silver wings against orange burnished sky,
Nevada evenings creep into my eyes.
Then yesterdays from yesteryears unwind
In tender rushes I have missed so much.
They resurrect old flames inside my mind.
I swear I feel the soft brush of your touch.

Nevada nights have slipped right through my hands.
But still they live inside love's shadow lands

Never Lost

If songs feel wrong and nothing moves your soul
I'll be your music, sing you melodies.
When all your diamonds turn back into coal
I'll find new jewels I know are sure to please.
When all is lost and you can't carry on,
And there be no repair for wounded pride;
When everyone you counted on is gone,
You'll find I'll still be standing by your side.
If you should feel your chest ache, breathing thin,
I'll cradle you and I will be your breath.
If you should feel a frost begin within,
I'll hold your hand and follow you through death

Wherever you may go I'll be there too;
You never will be lost. I will find you.

Fading Fingerprints

The last of Earthly life has disappeared.
The world engulfed in sea of silent sound
Inside this moment dreaded and so feared
That evidenced the violent death abound.
Inherited by fools, this poisoned wind,
It stopped their hearts from beating in their tracks.
These non environmentalists that sinned;
They paid no heed to facts or almanacs
That spurned the unforgiving wheel of fate
Beneath translucent, copper painted sky
And we were made to pay this price too great:
There's no one left to witness moons pass by;

Not one soul left alive to shed a tear;
Just fading fingerprints that we were here.

Summer Stone

A Summer stone holds dreams of Springtime past
And muses on the Autumn winds to come.
The sunlit skies of August never last.
September always puts them on the run,
But pebbles on this beach still strum the breeze
And some dreams never die they must abide.
Though Autumn forces Summer to its knees,
And chases leaves that run away and hide,
So I will keep this Summer stone with me
And zip it up inside my pocket tight.
I'll wish on it until my eyes can see
The embers of your eyes enflame my night.

If I could climb inside this Summer stone,
I'd be no more the texture of alone.

Angel Heart

Begone small speck that dares to cloud my eye
And threatens spilling out in shades of blue.
That I should think of you I must decry.
I spit these lies professing they are true.
I deign to be that most which I am not:
Parading through the world in false disguise
As one with cold heart never once besot,
Soul never fallen prey to passion's lies.
But if a tender heart wouldst dare attend,
Clad only in the essence of true love,
Too strong to break yet strong enough to bend,
And give my clipped heart wings to soar above,

We'd slay this trepidation haunting me.
Oh angel heart with wings, where can you be!

Fever

If fever overtaketh me this night
And draws me closer, drawing my last breath;
If Earthly shades droop down to dim the light
And reaper grim should come to claim my death,
Should I now welcome her with open arms
In drunkenness or feigned sobriety?
And was she also victim to your charms
Or did she smugly smirk in piety?
But matters not the fact or circumstance,
I'll rally; turn her back at heaven's gate.
Then clinging fast to life beg one more chance
To journey on toward my destined fate.

If there be God in heaven hear my prayer.
Ensure my love safe trip to meet me there.

Beguiled

Before, through yearning, longing, lovesick lens
My eyes beheld you in love's afterglow;
And though this self-delusion never ends,
The better part of me has come to know
The narcissistic flavour of your soul;
A bitter root that's sour to the core;
A shiny diamond heart that's only coal;
A wild tsunami crashing on love's shore;
The thunder rolls it has no other choice.
Naivity will crush a heart in love
That did not care to heed small warning voice
Of angel calling faintly from above.

The truth arrives disguised as vengeful child.
Too late for hapless heart thus so beguiled.

Design

Last night, perchance, a lady bug did fall.
With weary wings she lit down on my arm,
Aware of Autumn drums' approaching call,
The thrum of beat suggesting pending harm.
God's creatures large, to medium and small,
All dance within their sep'rate symphony.
They prance on dreams as melodies stand tall
Reverberating Nature's harmony.
But lady bug so far away from home
Was unaware her house may be on fire,
Til breeze did call through gossamer tooth comb
'Your children are alone on fune'ral pyre'.

With weary wings small creature flew away
While God designed to write another play.

The Dark

Surrounded by the darkened edge of gloom
I sit in trance now forced to see the truth;
How selfish misspent moments led to doom.
I now decry these failings of my youth.
So many roads I did not choose to walk.
So many dreams concerning me alone
Have disappeared like time and trite small talk
And I've become the dog without a bone.
In hindsight I discern the glass from gold,
Aware now of the jewel you offered me;
Your loyal loving heart to have and hold,
But in my youth this truth I could not see.

I walk in darkness searching for your light.
I must find you to end this endless night.

Vancouver

The Sun spills over snow capped sentinels,
Pries sleeping city eyelids open wide.
Downtown the sound of horns and tinkling bells.
A lonely seagull glides above the tide.
A city full of strangers on the street;
They hurry, scurry, go their sep'rate ways.
Exchanging quickened smiles they meet and greet.
They wend through this amazing maze of days:
A trip through busy mall, or to the park,
A gourmet meal at uptown eatery,
A neon flashlight gleaming in the dark,
Artistic palette splash of scenery.

Svelte condos, mountains, surf and turf and bars,
Vancouver sparkles bright beneath the stars.

Birds On A Wire

You touch my soul like blazing prairie fire;
Like morning dew on windblown desert rose.
Our wings electric, love birds on a wire,
Tips wrapt in passion as it sparks and glows.
The wire song pierces deep into our hearts
With mystic rhythm softly flowing through.
Inside these sacred canyons music starts
With notes from horn of plenty blending blue
Into a rhapsody of precious song.
Locked safely in each other's warm embrace,
At journey's end we are where we belong
We wipe the tears that stained each other's face.

On live wire, birds with burnt electric wings;
Electrocution savoured as love sings.

Ink Stain In The Rain

In sordid cave, a cruel wind scrapes and rapes
As we perform our tragic masquerade.
The edge of night stilettos through the drapes
Revealing shadows hiding in the shade.
In evil guise it breathes foreboding gloom.
I shiver hard to keep my body warm.
Beneath a brooding sky I sense the doom
And touch the trembling lip of sudden storm.
Waves rise I feel your heart begin to slip.
You drop my hand. The tide sweeps you away.
A stranger on the shore. A passing ship.
One born to stay. The other born to stray.

Love letters, pain's refrain, left in the rain.
What once was fire, is now a damp ink stain.

Folly

In everlasting quest of truthfulness,
I travelled through a forest rife with lies.
There, wrought with woe, the deeds I can't confess;
That haunt my thoughts between the pause of sighs.
Now further from my rest I travel on.
I step through corpses, search for pulsing beat,
Still searching for forgiveness dead and gone,
In quest of finding one last spark of heat
Rekindling hope to save my sordid soul.
I see redemption's rocky road ahead.
It leads to blessings I've been searching for.
My restitution made in deed and dread,
I'll beg on bended knee at heaven's door.

Here at the crossroads facing bitter truth,
I rue the folly of my misspent youth.

Chapters

So many chapters of my life now read
That seldom are revisited again,
But when I choose to resurrect the dead
And dance again with memories and pain
You're still the brightest star in my grey sky.
It matters not the heartaches you dispersed.
Some depths are measured by a shallow sigh.
Yes, there are some hearts born to be accursed.
Alas, when all seems lost we carry on
And vow we'll not reread that wistful book,
But when we least expect it comes a song
That brings to life old heartaches we forsook.

When leafing through those pages in the rain,
You're there in every bittersweet refrain.

Wraith Demons

A ghostly hawk perched high on boulder ledge,
With feathers proudly preened against blue sky,
His talons gripped a beating severed heart.
He stumbled losing balance at the edge.
Then flew this bird of prey to hunt my soul
And I to gather up my pistol whip.
This grisly demon, eyes as black as coal
Had not a beak but wore a human lip.
Decision broke the tumult in my mind.
I did not flee I chose to stand my ground.
Shunned cowardice was never of my kind.
My bullet found its mark with deaf'ning sound.

The hawk and severed heart from overhead
Fell bloodied at my feet. Wraith demons dead.

Relentless Reign

In this world, better loved you'll never be.
No one could hold you closer to their heart.
No one could place you higher in esteem
And thus it's been right from the very start.
Close up and red hot, swimming in your eyes,
I swore I saw love's treasures manifold.
The truth shone through. I came to realize
That I could not turn tin love into gold.
Your heart designed with razor sharpened knife
To slice mine in premeditated kill.
Yet, you remain the great love of my life.
This madness haunts me still! It always will.

I stand, a hollow statue wrought with pain,
Held under spell of love's relentless reign.

Albatross

He drew attention to the time of day.
Inside this darkened season of his soul,
He feigned to speak but knew not what to say.
She cocked her ear to hear the thunder roll
But none forthcoming, silence ruled the court.
As many issues reared their ugly head,
This was the final straw, the last resort.
Their albatross lay wingless on the bed.
And this is how iniquity abounds,
How hearts are cordoned off in private grief,
When paper lawyers search to find new grounds
To resurrect the dead and free the thief.

In search of diamonds at the edge of night,
Their albatross is fading from the light.

Sado-Masochistic Reveries

In sado-masochistic reveries
I try to claw my way back to your door.
I crawl back to your bed on bleeding knees
And beg to be mistreated ever more.
Your tender violence cuts like supple wire
With passion's forty lashes at the wall.
Cremation of the soul inside your fire,
I am the architect of my own fall.
But should psychoanalysis prevail
And drive all these perversions from my mind,
In masochistic moments I'd bewail
This happiness laid heavy on my mind.

So lay me down in love's sweet misery
And sado-masochistic reveries.

Lost

When I played music. You sang a cappella
And you believed the lie I spoke was true.
A million eyes to pierce night's dark umbrella,
To light my way but still I can't find you.
You're still enshrouded in that tender lie,
The one I swore to be the gospel truth,
And I'm so filled with guilt that I could cry
Forlorn within the folly of my youth.
Old sunsets try to creep inside my eyes.
As starlight fades and wanders far afield,
I chase old ghosts that dress in new disguise.
Alas, my fate was long ago thus sealed.

The essence of our serenade in blue
Has found my heart, but still I can't find you.

Sistine Sonnet

Inside a Sistine sonnet's heart there lies
A living ceiling dancing, in a dream
Of Michelangelo's soft brush and sighs,
Baptized with fire inside His sacred stream.
An inspiration, miracle divine
Within this realm for all the world to see;
An invocation of the Lord's design
A monument to His veracity.
Wouldst any devil dare to enter here
Where wisdom and compassion's brides reside?
The wrath of God doth still beget true fear.
The power of the Lord won't be denied.

This Sistine sonnet rings its chapel bell
To show the painted word God has to tell.

The Saving

Could I but feign to be the castle's knight
In match set game of never win checkmate?
I must escape this all consuming fate;
This double jeopardy in season trite.
A bruised messiah in demonic flight,
In devilish pursuit of fallen mate,
Outside the River Styx iron curtained gate
Where Lucifer unleashes Hellish blight.

But purest soul can turn wrought iron to pearl
And shine it into bright majestic dreams
That form the fabric of a magic glove
To gather all the goodness in the world
And turn it into purifying streams;
Destroying evil 'til there's only love.

No Choice

He's gone from crumpled carbon paper night.
Mere copy of a great love now grown faint.
His memory is fading out of sight.
His image peeling off me like old paint.
Is there a duplicate out there someplace?
And if there is, I need to track it down;
Destroy each remnant and remove all trace;
Submerge it's residue and watch it drown,
But if this rogue should fall down at my feet
To beg forgiveness for his wanton ways;
Foreswear and promise nevermore to cheat
But cleave to only me 'til end of days.

If he would forfeit life and love to me,
I'd have no choice but to accept his plea.

Fragrance

The sunlight fell through darkened sky's embrace.
That night of passion burned a brighter bold.
Eternity was ours to have and hold;
Then stardust sprinkled kisses on your face,
And suddenly we owned this sacred place.
Alive with dreams that can't be bought or sold
This feeling strengthened, growing manifold.
We swayed in acts of love and knew God's grace;

Then unexpected chill turned sun to shade.
The change came quickly. You left me behind.
I'm passion's orphan, love's lost refugee
But still I smell the fragrance of that glade;
That sweet aroma pungent in my mind,
And time cannot take that away from me.

Comparing The Trade

You dared like Eastwood saving Meryl Streep
And we were chic like Bogey and Bacall;
But fascination wasn't ours to keep
And we became the legends of our fall.
Like Burton and Liz Taylor tooth and nail
We drank and fought into delirium.
Love lost its innocence on heartache's trail
And shattered in our glass emporium;
But in each shard of glass I see your face
And long for passion's poison and your kiss.
I search for you in every ghost I chase.
The tally of my years has come to this:

I'd trade each hour spent in happiness
For one more chance to feel your sweet caress.

Tragic Masquerade

Your icy heart has brought me to my knees.
Your smile has burned to ashes in my mind;
And all the while inside this forlorn freeze,
The ink stains still aren't dried upon love's line.
Personifying narcissistic love
Could not outshine your wanton vanity.
Clad in illusion's magic slight of glove,
Love drove me past the point of sanity.
As maudlin moments spool and then unwind
The calloused hands of time turn back my heart.
Dark fingers of dank fog surround my mind.
It's yesterday again we're not apart.

The curtain falls; the final scene displayed;
I'm trapped inside this tragic masquerade.

These Brave Hearts

Commissioned poem for Remembrance Day ceremonies 2011

Courageously they marched forth into Hell
Amidst the gunfire, mortar shells, and death;
The brave hearts left there where their bodies fell
What name was on their lips at their last breath?
They have our admiration and respect
These architects of freedom; heroes all,
As teardrops fall old memories reflect
The brave young hearts that answered duty's call.
They gave their lives to keep the hounds at bay,
These saviors still remembered through the years.
A somber day, this day, Remembrance Day;
A day of courage, sacrifice and tears.

To these brave hearts we owe an unpaid debt;
The blood red poppy worn, "Lest We Forget".

We Dance In Darkness

I drift on silent waves at edge of sleep.
A hazy voice is chanting in my mind.
I rise in wisps of smoke to climb the steep
Of night and everywhere I look I find
A haunting melody of liquid flame
In black metallic corner of my world.
The voice is clearer now. You call my name
And beckon me into your arms unfurled.
In close embrace, I feel your breath on mine.
The atmosphere becomes electric air.
We spin together twinning on love's vine
And climb the slip'pry slope of heaven's stair.

Adrift in tangled smoke rings high above,
We dance in darkness to the end of love.

Beyond The Shadow Of The Veil

Beyond the shadow of the veil, I see
That my roads lead to you and yours to mine.
We're not the authors of our destiny
But players in God's grandiose design.
So many snow capped mountains we will climb
Beneath this tapestry of stardust skies.
We'll pass the pristine edge of tide and time,
Held safely in each other's breath and sighs.
My heart is handcuffed by your tender kiss;
Our spirits sewn together into one;
Your heart forever shackled to my wrist;
And as He wills it, so it will be done.

You are my ship. I am the sea you sail.
We're one beyond the shadow of the veil.

Sonnet Repast

Alone at table dressed in pantomime,
For pleasing meal of sonnet and red wine;
Iambic rhythm pulsing, keeping time,
I mused in syllables ten beats per line.
Pentameter adhered to lines thus stressed;
In candlelight the pages burned white hot.
Words took communion begging to be blessed.
The atmosphere was one of somber thought.
The yin and yang, the ebb and amber glow
Of metaphors that flowed from poet's fleece.
A symphony, a colourful Van Gogh,
The sonnet spilled in vivid masterpiece.

A poem was my choice of gourmet mood
And sonnet repast was my choice of food.

Midnight Embers

The fiery blaze before the burning out
Is recompense for what must come to pass.
When living in the shadow of a doubt
Becomes more fragile than the thinnest glass,
Then something has to give. A heart will break.
Like haunting songs with bittersweet refrain
It leaves behind an echo in its wake.
Love is not dead that does not die again,
And in these sessions love can't be denied.
The longing, yearning, passion, memory;
An old black magic pull, an ache inside;
The musing, gleaning of what used to be.

The magic spell these midnight embers cast
Restoke the fires and passions of the past.